THE WINNING EDGE

CATCHING

By BOB CLUCK

Foreword by LANCE PARRISH

CONTEMPORARY
BOOKS, INC.
CHICAGO • NEW YORK

Library of Congress Cataloging-in-Publication Data

Cluck, Bob.
    The winning edge : catching.

    1. Catching (Baseball)—Juvenile literature.
I. Title.
GV872.C55   1987   796.357'23   86-32939
ISBN 0-8092-4787-9 (pbk.)

All photos courtesy Teri Cluck Photography
Equipment courtesy San Diego School of Baseball

Published by Contemporary Books, Inc.
180 North Michigan Avenue, Chicago, Illinois 60601
Manufactured in the United States of America
Library of Congress Catalog Card Number: 86-32939
International Standard Book Number: 0-8092-4787-9

Published simultaneously in Canada by Beaverbooks, Ltd.
195 Allstate Parkway, Valleywood Business Park
Markham, Ontario L3R 4T8 Canada

To Teri, Jennifer, and Amber
for patience during the long road trips
and the film sessions at home
over 20 great years

Contents

Foreword 6
1. What Is a Good Catcher? 9
2. The Catcher's Equipment 13
3. Stances and Receiving the Ball 21
4. Throwing to the Bases 31
5. How to Make the Tag
at Home Plate 45
6. Blocking Pitches in the Dirt 55
7. Pop-Ups, Bunts, and Cutoffs 65
8. How to Help the Pitcher
Get Hitters Out 73
9. Practice, Practice, Practice 77
Index 78

Foreword

Catching is often thought of as the single most important position on the baseball field, often called "the field general" or "the quarterback" of the team. The catcher is directly involved in the handling of the entire pitching staff and is responsible for knowing the strengths and weaknesses of every hitter that steps up to the plate. When the pressure starts to mount in a game situation, it is the catcher who is expected to take control and keep the pitcher's energy and concentration centered on getting the job done and avoiding any distractions.

The physical aspect of catching requires total concentration on the fundamentals of the job. Just like anything else, you should work on the proper ways of doing things until they become second nature. First, get a glove that feels comfortable to you. Be sure to break it in properly before you decide to use it in a game. You don't want balls to be jumping out of your glove the entire game.

When you get behind the plate, try to get as comfortable as possible. Believe it or not, you *can* get into a comfortable position while catching. Make sure when you position yourself behind the hitter you allow enough room for the hitter to make his full swing without making contact with you or your glove. This way you'll avoid injury to yourself and interfering with the hitter's swing.

Once you find that right position, it's time to get yourself ready. Spread your feet about shoulder width apart so when you're in the squat position you are well balanced. Always stay on the balls of your feet so you are able to bounce and react quickly. Keep your shoulders square to the pitcher and give a good target after pitch selection has been made. If a ball is thrown in the dirt, try to block it—don't try to catch it. The main objective in this situation is to keep the ball in front of you and prevent it from going to the backstop.

When blocking a ball in the dirt, try to drop to both knees either to the left, to the right, or straight down in front of you. No matter which direction you drop, always keep your shoulders square to the pitcher's mound so the ball will stay in front of you and not kick off to the side. When you're on your knees, pull your arms in at your sides and position your glove between your knees to plug the gap between your legs. Keep your head looking down at the ball. The mask will protect you and prevent injury.

When throwing the ball to a base to prevent a steal, make sure to be on the balls of your feet before the ball has been pitched. You might want to drop your right foot back a little to be in more of a throwing position. Catch the ball, get a good grip on it, and try to feel for a seam so when you make your throw it is more accurate. Try not to rush your throw. Most of the time your mistakes are made when you rush things. A ball that is thrown on the money is going to get the runner more times than if you rush yourself and the throw is off a little bit.

On pop-ups, turn your back to the playing field and face the stands. The rotation on a pop-up will always make the ball come back to the playing field. If you face the stands, the ball will come to you, not away from you. Take your mask off and hold on to it. Get a fix on the ball and get into position, then throw your mask out of your way so you don't step on it and make the catch.

Best of luck.

Lance Parrish

1
What Is a
Good Catcher?

It is common knowledge that if a baseball team is to be a winner it must have solid pitching and defense. Nothing is more important to good defense than a good catcher, and most coaches will tell you that the single most important player on the team is the catcher. Over the years in the major leagues, no successful team has been without a fine defensive catcher. The Yankees of the 1950s and 1960s had Yogi Berra and Elston Howard, the Dodgers of the same era had Roy Campanella and John Roseboro. Other examples are the Reds of the 1970s with Johnny Bench, and the Mets and Angels of the 1980s with Gary Carter and Bob Boone, respectively.

The catcher must be a team leader, direct the efforts of the pitchers, and in many ways become an extension of the coach or manager. The catcher must be an enthusiastic player who is durable, dependable, and who displays a positive attitude at all times. He must be able to separate his offense and defense. A spectator who arrives at the ballpark late in the game and watches the catcher on defense should not be able to tell if he is 4 for 4 at the bat or 0 for 4.

A good catcher should work with his pitchers and develop a personal relationship with each one of them. He must quickly learn which ones to "chew out," and which ones to "stroke." To get the most out of each pitcher, the catcher must find out which ones are weak emotionally and which are strong. The weak will need constant attention, while the strong usually can be left alone. He must learn the delivery of each pitcher, and be able to tell when something is wrong.

A GOOD CATCHER

▶ Is a team leader.
▶ Has a positive attitude.
▶ Is an enthusiastic player (almost a cheerleader).
▶ Is tough and durable and handles minor injuries like a professional.
▶ Works well with his pitchers.
▶ Has a special relationship with the coach and/ or manager.
▶ Gets along with the umpires.
▶ Has a professional approach to the game at all times.

The bottom line is that there just aren't enough good defensive catchers, even in the major leagues. The position requires exceptional athletic skills and a special attitude toward the game. Most players aren't willing to pay the price.

2
The Catcher's Equipment

THE CATCHER'S GLOVE

A lightweight, flexible glove is recommended for all young players. You must be sure-handed and be able to get the ball out of your glove easily when a throw is necessary. In other words, your glove must fit; you should not have to "grow into" a catcher's glove.

Use a lightweight, flexible glove that allows you to get the ball out easily when throwing.

13

THE CATCHER'S MASK, HELMET, AND THROAT GUARD

The mask is your best friend. You should inspect it regularly for damage and always use a mask with protective "ears." Some catchers get into the bad habit of turning their heads when the hitter swings, and these "ears" help protect the side of the head. Even after you learn not to shy away, the ears help protect against the catcher's nemesis, the foul tip. An experienced catcher quickly learns that all of his protection is on the front of his body.

A catcher's helmet is a necessity, and more and more catchers are using them today. Because some catchers drop their heads when catching low pitches (especially when the hitter swings), a helmet is very important to protect the top of the head. In addition, some hitters will let go of the bat with one hand and accidentally hit the catcher with it during the follow-through. This can cause serious injury, and a helmet will obviously help.

Several years ago the Dodgers developed a throat guard for catchers that has saved many a catcher from foul tips. Even if you keep your chin down well, your throat is still vulnerable to foul tips. Even balls that bounce first still hurt a lot, and at least one youth league catcher has died from such an injury (the windpipe can swell and restrict the flow of oxygen).

The protective "ears" on the mask help protect you from foul tips (note the less expensive mask without the "ears").

Catchers drop their heads when receiving low pitches, so a helmet will protect the top of the head.

A helmet will protect you if you should get hit with the bat after the swing.

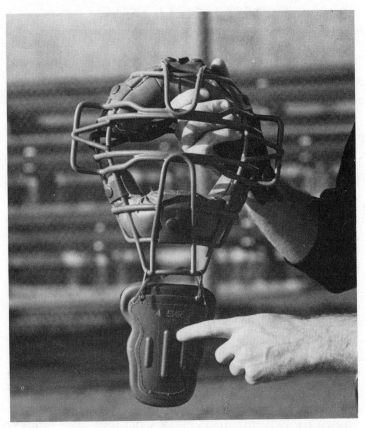

A throat guard should be standard equipment for all catchers at all levels.

THE CHEST PROTECTOR, PROTECTIVE CUP, AND SHIN GUARDS

Your chest protector and shin guards should fit well. Equipment that is either too big or too small creates more chance for injury than it is designed to prevent. Shin guards that are too small won't protect the kneecaps, and if they are too big you can't run or move effectively. Oversize shin guards can make a catcher trip and fall while fielding bunts, backing up bases, or running after pop-ups. The shin guards should be fastened on the outside of the leg so they don't get caught while you're running.

A supporter and protective cup should be worn by every player from Little League to the major leagues. It's a mandatory piece of equipment for all catchers. The risks of permanent injury are just too great without it. It's uncomfortable at first, but this is only temporary. It can be worth its weight in gold when that one bad hop or foul tip comes your way. At the higher levels, a catcher will get hit several times a season, and with pitchers throwing harder and harder, even in Little League, you're foolish not to wear this protection. Protective cups should be worn in practice as well as in games.

PROPER EQUIPMENT FOR A CATCHER

▶ A lightweight, flexible catcher's glove
▶ A catcher's mask with protective "ears"
▶ A catcher's helmet
▶ A throat guard to protect against foul tips
▶ An athletic supporter and protective cup
▶ Shin guards and chest protector that fit (with guards fastened on the outside)

Your equipment should fit properly for maximum protection and proper execution of skills.

19

3
Stances and Receiving the Ball

THE PRIMARY OR "SIGN-GIVING" STANCE

When giving signs, you assume the position that is best described as the primary stance. Your glove hand is in a position that will prevent the third-base coach from seeing the signs. The position of your right knee will prevent the first-base coach from seeing them. To hide the signs from the opponents' dugout, keep your hand in a position that is neither too low nor too high. Place your right thumb on top of your protective cup and extend the fingers from there.

The kind of signs you give are unimportant, but you should use the same signs for all the pitchers on the staff. The key is to keep them simple so everyone can understand (one finger for a fastball,

21

two for a curveball, three for changeup, and a fist for a pitchout are common).

With a runner on second base the signs must be disguised in some manner. Giving three signs and having the pitcher use the middle sign or the last sign is the usual system.

The relaxed stance for giving signs (notice position of right hand).

The first-base coach is prevented from viewing signs by the proper positioning of your right knee.

The glove is used to block the vision of the third-base coach.

Some catchers have adopted a style with one leg extended; this is used to give a lower sign, but is not necessarily recommended.

THE SECONDARY OR "RECEIVING" STANCE

After you give the signs, you must shift from the relaxed primary position to the "ready" or "receiving" position. You can "walk" into this position by first moving your left foot and then the right. Your right foot is positioned three or four inches behind the left to allow for freedom of movement and quickness. The toe of your right foot will line up with the instep of the left. Your thighs should be parallel to the ground and your back straight. Your glove hand should be nearly extended and not "trapped" between your knees. Your weight should be slightly forward on the balls of your feet. Even though this position may seem awkward at first, it will soon become comfortable and workable. You must be able to move in all directions quickly, and this position enables you to do this easily. Your bare hand should be behind you with no one on base, but in a ready-to-throw position with men on base.

You should be in a position that seems a little close to the hitter. This helps in avoiding foul tips and in catching low strikes and blocking balls in the dirt (you're closer to the bounce).

This is the stance that catchers use to make throws, block pitches, and perform all of their other skills.

The "receiving" stance allows you to move laterally with maximum quickness (notice that the bare hand is behind you in a nobody-on-base situation).

Your weight should be on the balls of your feet, with your back straight and with your glove hand nearly extended (notice the position of the bare hand in a men-on-base situation). Set up in a position fairly close to the hitter to avoid some of the foul tips. This position will also help you catch the low strike and block pitches in the dirt.

GIVING A TARGET

When you assume the "ready" or "receiving" position, give the pitcher a target to help him throw strikes. The target (in the lower-level leagues) should be down the middle and low (about knee high on the hitter). Inexperienced pitchers should not be trying to throw to spots or locations when they have their hands full just throwing a strike. Later, a pitcher can "work" a hitter and "set him up" for different pitches in different locations.

4
Throwing to the Bases

Your catching ability is judged for the most part on your throwing strength and accuracy. Other parts of your game are certainly important, but throwing is the measure by which your peers and opponents will rate you on defense.

Throwing accurately depends on a combination of preparation and mechanics. The first step in preparation is to be comfortable in the receiving stance. Second, you must be constantly thinking when runners are on base. A throwing situation can develop at any time, and the catcher who is prepared mentally will be able to react properly. Situations such as possible steals of second, third, or home can develop. A well-timed pickoff play can save a team in a difficult situation.

You should never watch the flight of the ball after you throw. Instead, watch the target all the way. The ball will appear in your line of sight soon enough.

THROWING TO FIRST BASE

Pickoff plays to first base can be initiated by the catcher, first baseman, or the coach or manager. A sign is first given by one or the other and an acknowledgement is usually given in return. If a runner is caught leaning toward second, he is easy pickings for a well-executed pickoff.

A pitch on the outside half of the plate is best to throw on, so it is wise for you to set your target on the outside for that pitch. If the pitch is inside, it becomes difficult to throw, and it is best to abort the attempted pickoff.

Stay low, move your right foot early (even before catching the ball), and step with the left foot to make the throw.

When throwing to first, stay low and step with the right foot toward first base.

Throwing to the Bases

Close off your upper body by moving both hands across the top of the right thigh until your left shoulder is "closed."

Once you rotate your upper body, step in the direction of first base with the left foot (notice that you should stay low during the entire throw).

THROWING TO SECOND BASE

When a runner tries to steal second, the first baseman should help you out by yelling "There he goes!" when the runner breaks. Of course, you anticipate this situation and should be prepared to throw when the runner goes. The basic mechanics involve taking a small step with your right foot bringing your arms up across your chest, and taking a step with your left foot toward the target. During these steps, you should remain as low as possible.

Pitches in Different Areas

Because the location of the pitch is unpredictable, you must have a slightly different approach for each pitch in a different area. Practice receiving pitches and making throws from various pitch locations.

When the pitch is inside, take an early step with your left foot, shift your weight to your right foot, close off your front side by moving both hands across the letters, then step toward the target (second base) with your left foot. This movement (shifting left-right-left) is called the "click" method because the heels appear to click as you shift your weight.

Throwing to the Bases

On a pitch down the middle or to the outside, step to approximately a 45-degree angle with your right foot, close off your front side, and step toward second base with your left foot.

Throwing to the Bases

On a pitchout to a left-handed hitter take a longer step into the right-handed batter's box, shift your weight to the right foot as you close off your front side, and step toward second base with your left foot; be careful not to overthrow on a pitchout.

With a right-handed hitter at the plate, the pitchout goes to the left-handed batter's box; take a step with your right foot to "center" the ball on your left shoulder, close off your front side, then take a step toward second with your left foot.

THROWING TO THIRD BASE

When a hitter steals third, he usually steals it on the pitcher. With a left-handed hitter up, your throw is much easier and involves a step with your left foot toward the target (some catchers elect to take an early step toward the ball with the right foot and then step toward the base with the left foot). When a right-handed hitter is up, you must decide whether you're going to throw in front of or behind the hitter. The pitch will dictate which direction you should go. When the pitch is outside, throw in front of the hitter by taking a step forward with your right foot, and then stepping toward third with your left foot. When the pitch is down the middle or on the inside, take a step to the side with your left foot, shift your weight to the right foot, and take a step toward third with your left foot. (Remember that the hitter moves toward the pitcher when he strides, and clearing for the throw will be easier than it appears.)

With a right-handed hitter, the throw to third is more difficult, and you must decide whether to throw behind or in front of the hitter; the location of the pitch will dictate the direction in which you should go.

Throwing to the Bases

When the pitch is outside, throw in front of the hitter by taking a step to the ball with your right foot and then step toward third with your left foot.

Check the runner on third before throwing to second on a possible double steal of second and home.

THE FIRST-AND-THIRD DOUBLE STEAL

When a team attempts to steal second with men on first and third, you must assume that a double steal is a possibility. Check the runner on third as you "close off" your front side in case he breaks. Then throw to second to get the base stealer attempting to steal second. If the runner on third breaks, the second baseman or the shortstop will come forward, catch the ball, and throw it back to home for the tag. When you check the runner initially and see that he has broken for the plate early, you throw him out or get him in a rundown. Remember that you always want to tag out the "lead" runner first.

SOME RULES TO REMEMBER ABOUT THROWING

- ▶ Don't rush; you will only mishandle the ball or make an inaccurate throw.
- ▶ The steps and other movements must be practiced over and over to gain consistency.
- ▶ Remain as low as possible and resist the tendency to "pop up" too soon.
- ▶ "Close off" your front side completely, or you will fly open too soon and throw the ball high.
- ▶ Watch the target and not the ball in flight.
- ▶ A quick, accurate throw will get the job done; trying to throw too hard will cause a major breakdown in mechanics and accuracy.

5
How to Make the Tag at Home Plate

Even though you wear protective equipment, serious injury can result if you apply tags improperly. The runner is coming in at full speed, and in any collision both you and the runner are going to lose. Most catchers take their masks off to make the tag, but it is perfectly acceptable to leave it on.

POSITIONING FOR THE TAG

You must learn how to block the plate to be an effective tagger. There have been a few catchers in history who were great at blocking the plate. The best was probably Johnny Bench of the Cincinnati

45

Reds. Another who comes to mind is Mike Scioscia of the Los Angeles Dodgers. You must give the runner some of the plate to slide to or his only choice will be to run over you. Place your left foot with the toe pointing toward third base approximately 18 inches in front of home plate. This planted foot becomes what is called the "anchor" foot. The right foot becomes the "pivot" foot, as it will move around to position you to receive the throw without your having to leave the tagging position. Of course, if the ball is out of the tagging area, you will have to go get it. IT IS EXTREMELY IMPORTANT TO HAVE YOUR LEFT FOOT POINTING TOWARD THE RUNNER WHEN HE IMPACTS THE LEG. Your knee will bend without damage if it bends straight back. However, if your knee is forced to bend sideways, it can suffer interior or exterior ligament damage that may require surgery to repair.

After placing your left foot in the initial position, and upon catching the ball, move your left foot to block the plate entirely (the runner has committed to the slide at this point). The runner will slide into your left foot and be stopped from reaching home plate (remember that your toe is still pointing toward the runner at impact).

As you apply the tag, the back of your glove should always be toward the runner to avoid injury to the inside of your wrist. After the tag you should alertly look around for another play.

How to Make the Tag at Home Plate

Place your left foot about 18 inches in front of home plate and point your toe toward third base. The left foot is called the "anchor" foot.

Upon catching the ball, you place your bare hand over it and leave it in your bare hand throughout the tagging process.

After catching the ball, move your left foot to block the plate (the runner has committed to the slide at this point).

As you apply the tag, move your hands apart to reduce the chance of the ball being jarred loose (notice that the back of your glove should be toward the runner).

WHEN THE RUNNER IS TRYING TO SCORE STANDING UP

If the runner is coming in standing up, you should try to avoid the collision. When the throw arrives, place your right hand over the ball (the ball will remain in your bare hand) and at contact simply roll with the tag counterclockwise. Separate your hands at contact to reduce the danger of having the ball jarred loose. After the tag look around for another play.

Avoid a severe collision by rolling the tag in a counterclockwise direction (notice the ball in the bare hand).

51

If the throw is slightly off line, move your right foot, or "pivot" foot, to the ball without leaving the solid tagging position.

When the throw is way off line, you must leave your tagging position and get the ball.

WHAT TO REMEMBER ABOUT TAG PLAYS AT THE PLATE

- ▶ Your initial position should allow the runner to see some of the plate.
- ▶ The ball is held in the bare hand to make the tag, and the back of the glove is toward the runner at all times.
- ▶ As you receive the ball, move your left foot, or "anchor" foot to block the plate entirely.
- ▶ The toe of your left foot should point up the line toward the runner and third base.
- ▶ Avoid collisions at the plate if at all possible, with or without protective gear; everyone loses in a severe collision.
- ▶ Be alert and look for another play after the tag.

6
Blocking Pitches in the Dirt

One of your important jobs is to block pitches in the dirt. Every pitcher will throw pitches in the dirt during the course of a game, and few catchers can block them all. One of the keys is anticipation. When you have a pitcher who throws lots of curveballs in the dirt, look for each curveball he calls to be thrown low. There is a different method used to block each of the three different pitches that a catcher must block.

BALLS IN THE DIRT AND OVER THE PLATE

The ball straight at you is the easiest to block; it involves simply dropping to both knees directly at

55

the ball. Your chin should be tucked, and your glove should protect your groin and stop the ball that could escape between your legs. Your upper body should "hover" over the ball by leaning forward as far as possible. This movement will direct the ball back toward the ground and prevent it from rolling too far away. Your body should center on the ball and be perpendicular to its flight. The object is to direct the ball toward the middle of the diamond to prevent any runners from advancing. Chances are that as long as the ball remains in front of you, the runners will not try to advance.

When you try to catch the ball instead of blocking it, you open an avenue for escape between your legs.

Blocking Pitches in the Dirt

To block pitches in the dirt directly at you, drop to both knees and lean forward, with your chin tucked against your chest.

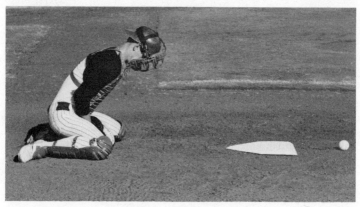

BALLS IN THE DIRT TO EITHER SIDE

For blocking pitches to either side, use the same basic blocking position. The difference is in the initial movements to arrive at the blocking position. Use the opposite leg to drive off of (right leg to go left, left leg to go right). You must also make an attempt to get around to block the ball straight back toward the pitcher. If the angle is improper, the ball will take a path away from the center of the diamond, and runners will advance.

Blocking Pitches in the Dirt

When the ball is to the left, drive off your right leg and drop to both knees (notice that the angle of your body blocks the ball back toward the middle of the diamond).

CATCHING

Drive off your left leg when the ball is to your right (notice the body lean, chin tuck, and glove position).

Blocking Pitches in the Dirt

CATCHING

After you block the ball, get to your feet, get rid of your mask, and prepare to throw if a runner is attempting to advance.

A failure to block a ball at a critical time can put a runner in scoring position, allow him to go to third, let him score an easy run. Even letting a runner move to second in the first inning can eventually cost your team the game. You won't improve at this skill unless you practice hard. The pain comes with the job, and bruises are a part of being a catcher. Practice blocking tennis or rubber balls at first, and after you learn the mechanics, you can introduce baseballs.

There is no greater feeling for a catcher than to block a tough curveball in the dirt with the winning run on third in the final inning. Catching is a difficult position, and blocking balls is the single toughest skill you must master.

HOW TO BLOCK BALLS SUCCESSFULLY

▶ Assume a balanced position from which quick movements are possible.
▶ Anticipate the ball in the dirt.
▶ Drop to both knees and assume an angle that is perpendicular to the path of the ball.
▶ Center on the ball by trying to make it hit you dead center in your chest protector.
▶ Tuck your chin to protect your throat.
▶ Lean over the ball with your upper body to direct it toward the ground.
▶ Drive off the opposite leg when making a block to the side.
▶ Resist the tendency to try to catch the ball; instead block it by placing your glove in the opening between your legs and leaving it there.

7

Pop-Ups, Bunts, and Cutoffs

CATCHING POP-UPS

Pop-ups can give you fits if you don't have an effective system to catch them. The ball comes off the bat spinning violently and will curve back toward the middle of the field as it comes down. When the ball leaves the bat, you should turn your back on home plate in order to keep the ball in front of you. As the ball rises, give chase with mask in your hand. When the ball reaches its highest point, throw the mask away, being careful not to overrun the ball (remember that the ball will curve back toward you as it comes down).

Catch the ball over your head and not with a basket catch. Establish your area of responsibility for pop-up coverage. You should have priority on balls behind the plate, and give the right-of-way to the first and third basemen on balls near the dugouts.

*Keep the mask in your hand until you're positive
you know where the ball is.*

Catch the ball over your head with two hands.

FIELDING BUNTS

When the ball is bunted in front of the plate, you are in the best position to field it and make an accurate throw. When the ball is in your area of responsibility, you should call for it loudly and be aggressive as you approach it. If the ball is out of your area, help direct traffic and call the player who is to take the bunt. You should also call out the base that the ball should be thrown to.

While the ball is still rolling, field the ball with two hands and "scoop" it with your bare hand into the glove. The only time the ball should be fielded bare-handed is if it has completely stopped.

It is a good idea to keep the ball in front of you at all times. By circling the ball, you can go directly toward the base that you will be throwing to.

If the ball is in the immediate area of the plate, take a couple of steps out in front of the plate to "clear" the batter. Even though the batter must stay within the baseline according to the rules, many run inside this line. If you hit him with the throw, the umpire often won't see that the batter has left the baseline, and the defense is penalized.

To field the bunt directly in front of the plate or up the first-base line, take a direct route.

When the bunt is up the third-base line, circle the ball and head directly toward the base that you're throwing to.

DIRECTING CUTOFFS

You are the captain of the defense and should direct the efforts of the infielders on cutoffs and relays. When the ball is coming to the plate, it is important for you to know the speed of the runners. In addition, it is essential that you always know the score and what each runner represents. In most cases, if there isn't a good shot at getting the runner at the plate, the ball should be cut off to prevent the batter from advancing to scoring position.

Most teams use a simple system of voice communication. It doesn't matter which system you use as long as everyone on the team is in tune with the commands. Shouting "Cut!" to cut the ball off or "Relay!" to have the ball relayed is popular. Most teams don't say anything if they want the ball to come through to the catcher for the attempted tag at the plate.

8
How to Help the Pitcher Get Hitters Out

Most pitchers don't think well on the mound and quite simply need help. They will get flustered when things don't go well for them, they will battle the umpire on close pitches, and they will lose their mechanics as they overthrow pitch after pitch.

You as the catcher must be able to settle a pitcher down when he is losing emotional control. You must smooth things over with the umpire who is tired of the pitcher complaining on close pitches, and you must help the pitcher with his mechanics before he is out of the game and the team is losing by six runs.

PITCH SELECTION

Here are a few types of hitters, and the rules that generally apply to them. But remember, there are exceptions to every rule, and you must watch each hitter carefully. Since there are no hard and fast rules, the pitcher and catcher must adjust if they are not successful with a particular "game plan."

Types of Hitters and Strategies to Get Them Out

Type of Hitter: Big, strong, tries to pull everything

Strategy: Throw him anything on the outside corner, or off-speed pitches anywhere

Type of Hitter: Crowds the plate

Strategy: Pitch him away (chances are he moved close to the plate because he doesn't handle the outside pitch well)

Type of Hitter: Stands way off the plate

Strategy: Pitch him inside because he probably doesn't handle the inside pitch well

Type of Hitter: Runs fast but without power

Strategy: Throw him nothing but strikes (the worst thing to do is walk him)

Type of Hitter: Has a severe uppercut

Strategy: Pitch him high fastballs

CATCHING

SETTING UP HITTERS

Most hitters fall into one of several categories, and a catcher must be able to spot differences in individual hitters and pitch them accordingly. With all hitters, the pitcher will have the most success when he gets ahead on the count and stays there. It is a fact that all hitters hit for a higher average when they are ahead on the count 2 and 0, or 3 and 1. It is important that regardless of pitch selection or location, the first pitch be a strike.

The pitcher and catcher must work together, but the catcher must remember that the ultimate choice of what to throw is the pitcher's. He is the one who must make the final decision on pitch selection, and the catcher really just makes suggestions in the form of signs.

9
Practice, Practice, Practice

No one has ever become a great ballplayer without practicing—and practicing hard. All the stars you see on the field, from Gary Carter and Bob Boone to Lance Parrish and Rich Gedman, got to where they are by digging in and working hard on the fundamentals.

A catcher has a big responsibility, and your teammates will be relying on you to be prepared for all possible situations. Here are some tips you can use so you'll always be ready for action:

▶ Set aside a certain time to practice every day.
▶ Get a friend, parent, or coach to practice with you. They can tell you what you're doing right or wrong.
▶ Review the parts of this book that deal with fundamentals that might be giving you trouble.

Finally, just remember to hang in there. With hard work and discipline, you'll be on your way to winning and becoming the best on the field!

Index

Anchor foot, 46, 54, *illus.* 47
Anticipation, 55
Athletic supporter, 19

Balls
  overrunning of, 65
Baselines
  running out of, 68
Bases
  backing up, 18
Bats
  hit by, 14
Batter
  clearing of, 68
  hitting during bunt, 68
Bench, Johnny, 9, 45
Berra, Yogi, 9
Blocking balls, 26
  failure to, 62
  how to, 63
  in the dirt, 55–63
  over the plate, 55–57,
    illus. 56, 57
  to either side, 58–62,
    illus. 59, 60, 61
  vs. catching, 56, 63
Boone, Bob, 9, 77
Bruises, 62
Bunts
  fielding of, 18, 68–70,
    illus. 69, 70

California Angels, 9
Calling for the ball, 68
Calling out the base, 68

Campanella, Roy, 9
Carter, Gary, 9, 77
Catchers
  defensive, 11
  good, 11
  job of, 9–10
Catches
  basket, 65
Catching balls
  vs. blocking of, 56, 63
Changeups, 22
Chest protectors, 18, 19, 63
Chin
  protection of, 14, 56, 63
Cincinnati Reds, 9, 45–46
Click method, 34, *illus.* 35
Closing off, 43, 44
Coaches, 9, 32, 77
  first-base, 21
  third-base, 21
Collisions, 45, 51, 54
Communication
  on the field, 71
Consistency, 44
Counts
  getting ahead on, 76
Curveballs, 22, 55
  blocking of, 62
Cutoffs
  directing of, 71

Death
  from injuries, 14
Defense, 9
  captain of, 71

Index

Dugouts
  opponents, 21
  right-of-way to, 65

Equipment, 5, 13–19, 54,
  illus. 19

Falling, 18
Fastballs, 21
Fielding
  bare-handed, 68
First baseman, 32
Foot
  anchor, 46, 54, *illus.* 47
  pivot, 46, *illus.* 52
Foul tips, 14, 26

Game plans, 74
Gedman, Rich, 77
Glove hand, 21, 26
Gloves, 13, 19, 56, *illus.* 13
  during tag, 46
Groin
  protection of, 56

Helmets, 14–17, 19, *illus.*
  15, 17
Hitters
  right-handed, 40
  setting up of, 29, 76
  spotting differences in,
    76
  types of, 75
  working of, 29
Hovering, 56
Howard, Elston, 9

Injuries, 14, 18, 45

Knee
  protection during slide,
    46
Kneecaps
  protection of, 18

Ligament damage, 46
Los Angeles Dodgers, 9, 14, 46

Managers, 32
Masks, 14–17, 19, 45, 62,
  illus. 15
  when to throw away, 65
New York Mets, 9
New York Yankees, 9

Overruning balls, 65
Oxygen
  lack of, 14

Pain, 62
Parrish, Lance, 77
Pickoff plays, 31, 32
Pitchers, 55, 58
  delivery of, 10
  helping, 73–76
  inexperienced, 29
Pitches
  close, 73
  handling during stealing
    attempts, 34, *illus.*
    35, 36, 37, 38
  location of, 76
  low, 14
  outside, 40
  overthrowing, 73
  selection of, 74–75, 76
Pitching, 9
  mechanics of, 73
Pitchouts, 22
  to left-hand hitters, *illus.* 38
  to right-hand hitters,
    illus. 39
Pivot foot, 46, *illus.* 52
Plate
  blocking of, 45–46
Pop-ups
  catching of, 65–67, *illus.*
    66, 67
  chasing, 18

CATCHING

Positions
  blocking, 58
Practice, 18, 62, 77
Protection, 14
Protective cups, 18, 19, 21

Receiving, 21–28
Relays, 71
Roseboro, Johnny, 9
Rundowns, 43
Runners
  caught leaning, 32
  lead, 43
  speed of, 71
Rushing, 44

Scioscia, Mike, 46
Score, 71
Shin Guards, 18, 19
Signs, 26, 76
  giving of, 21
  hiding of, 21
  pickoff, 32
  seeing, 21
Stances, 21–28, *illus.* 23,
    24, 25
  primary, 21–25
  receiving, 26–28, 31,
    illus. 27, 28
  relaxed, *illus.* 22
  secondary, 26–28
  "sign-giving," 21–25
Stealing, 31
  first-and-third double,
    43, *illus.* 42, 43
  second base, 34, 43
  third base, 40–42
Strategies
  for pitching to different
    types of hitters, 75
Strikes, 29
  low, 26

Surgery, 46

Tags, 71
  applying, 46
  at home plate, 44–52,
    illus. 47, 48, 49, 50,
    51, 52, 53
  positioning for, 45–49,
    illus. 47
  rolling with, 51
  rules for, 54
  stand-up, 51, *illus.* 51, 52
Target
  giving a, 29
Thinking, 73
Throat
  protection of, 63
Throat guards, 14–17, 19,
    illus. 17
Throwing
  accuracy of, 31
  rules for, 44
  strength of, 31
  to bases, 31–44
  to first base, 32–33, *illus.*
    32, 33
  to second base, 34–39,
    illus. 35, 36, 37, 38,
    39
  to third base, 40–42,
    illus. 41, 42
Throws
  accurate, 68
Traffic
  directing, 68
Tripping, 18

Umpires, 68, 73

Watching
  flight vs. target of ball,
    31